# A Place Called Home

## COUNT YOUR BLESSINGS

RACINE, WI

*A Place Called Home*
ISBN: 979-8-88898-007-1 - *Paperback*
ISBN: 979-8-88898-008-8 - *Hardcover*
ISBN: 978-1-970103-44-1 - *Ebook*
Copyright © 2022 by Honor Books

# INTRODUCTION

From the moment we are welcomed into this world until we breathe our final breath, "home" represents all that we need and long for. Sometimes those needs and longings are frustrated, but as we count the blessings of "home" and "family" our eyes are opened to treasures we hadn't seen. As Melody Beattie says, "Gratitude unlocks the fullness of life. It turns what we have into enough, and more. . . It can turn a meal into a feast, a house into a home . . ."

A friend told me about the "home" he had when he lived in Europe during World War II. The family, his mother and younger brother, moved constantly from place to place, from hotel to inn to a friend's home and back to a hotel again. Each time they would arrive, his mother would open the small suitcase filled with all their belongings and bring out the lace tablecloth that she had used for the Friday night meal in their home in Poland, before they were forced to leave and begin their travels.

In each place the ritual was exactly the same. She would place the suitcase on a table, carefully drape the tablecloth over the suitcase, light a candle, and in that moment, the place, wherever it was, became HOME.

SUE BENDER

# HOME

... THERE'S NO PLACE LIKE IT

Through the years, these words from the beloved poet . . . have sparked in me an amused and under- standing attitude—as I have watched the family come home, one by one—happy or sad, angry or "hyper," fighting or withdrawn. Anyone who lives in a family knows the many moods that cross the thresholds of our homes each day, but because we are a "colony of caring," we open the door, hold out our arms and we love!

ARVELLA SCHULLER

"When I was a boy in my father's house, still tender, and an only child of my mother, he taught me and said, 'lay hold of my words with all your heart; keep my commands and you will live.'"

PROVERBS 4:3-4

The Bible does not say very much about homes; it says a great deal about the things that make them. It speaks about life and love and joy and peace and rest. If we get a house and put these into it, we shall have secured a home.

JOHN HENRY JOWETT

I love houses that have the flotsam and jetsam of well-lived lives trailing from every surface. I love houses that have phone numbers and children's heights written on the walls, and heaps of seashells on the window sills, and skis stuck in the corner and ironing boards open in the kitchen. I love houses with crazy hats hanging from a hat stand, and cupids painted above the bathroom sink, and wisps of crepe paper peeling from being thumbtacks stuck in the wall, and pineapple tops growing in saucers.

NANCY EBERLE

It takes a heap o' livin' in a house
to' make it home,
A heap o' sun an' shadder, an' ye sometimes
have to' roam Afore ye really 'predate the
things ye lef' behind,
An' hunger fer 'em somehow, with 'em allus
on yer mind.

EDGAR A. GUEST

"Home is the place where, when you have
to go there, they have to take you in."

ROBERT FROST

When friends enter a home, they sense its personality and character, the family's style of living—these elements make a house come alive with a sense of identity, a sense of energy, enthusiasm, and warmth, declaring, "This is who we are; this is how we live."

RALPH LAUREN

"Home is where we start from," T.S. Eliot observed. Today, a century after he was born, "home" is the place where many women are longing to return, if not literally, then figuratively. Begin believing that the time, energy, and emotion you invest daily in the soulcraft of home-caring—carving out a haven for yourself and those dear to you—is a sacred endeavor.

SARAH BAN BREATHNACH

A house is a place where someone else lives. A home is my home.

LISA, AGE 11

Home is where they understand you.

CHRISTIAN MORGENSTERN

Before this altar crowned with peace,
This centre of our spirit home,
Let every strife and question cease
And Fruitful Faith and concord come.

For here the last deliverance stands,
To loose the palsied spell of fear;
And woman with unfettered hands
Keeps thine accepted priesthood here.

JULIA WARD HOWE

This world looks to us the natural and simple one, and so it is—absolutely fitted to our need and education. But there is that in us which is not at home in this world, which I believe holds secret relations with every star, or perhaps rather, with that in the heart of God whence issued every star, diverse in kind and character as in color and place and motion and light. To that in us, this world is so far strange and unnatural and unfitting, and we need a yet homelier home. Yea, no home at last will do, but the home of God's heart.

GEORGE MACDONALD

'Mid pleasures and palaces though we may roam,
Be it ever so humble, there's no place like home;
A charm from the sky seems to hallow us there,
Which, seek through the world, is ne'er met with
elsewhere.

How sweet 'tis to sit 'neath a fond father's smile.
And the caress of a mother to soothe and beguile!
Let others delight mid new pleasures to roam,
But give me, oh, give me, the pleasures of home!

Home, home, sweet, sweet home!
There's no place like home!
There's no place like home!

JOHN HOWARD PAYNE

Ah! There's nothing like staying home for real comfort.

JANE AUSTEN

Give me your tired, your poor,
Your huddled masses yearning to breathe free,
The wretched refuse of your teeming shore,
Send these, the homeless, tempest-tossed to me,'
I lift my lamp beside the golden door!

EMMA LAZARUS

When I was at home, I was in a better place.

WILLIAM SHAKESPEARE

Write it down, when I have perished:
Here is everything I've cherished;
That these walls should glow with beauty
Spurred my lagging soul to duty;
That there should be gladness here
Kept me toiling, year by year . . .
Every thought and every act
Were to keep this home intact.

EDGAR A. GUEST

What I really love about home is you don't have to pay for your dinner.

DAVID, AGE 11

I'd rather have roses on my table, than diamonds on my neck.

EMMA GOLDMAN

After a friend's mother died, there was a small amount of insurance money to be divided among the grown children. She and her siblings didn't want to drift apart, but they knew they'd have to make an effort to stay close since everyone lived so far from each other. They created a reunion fund to pay for lodging and food so that everyone could get together each summer. She says it was the first few reunions that were so crucial; after that, a new family tradition had been established. Now my friend feels closer to her brothers and sisters as an adult than she ever did as a child.

SARAH BAN BREATHNACH

# HOME

## IS FAMILY

What is a family? To the positive believer, it is a colony of caring—two or more individuals caring very deeply for each other. A family, then, is a group of people who, when you hurt, show that they care. You know they care!

ARVELLA SCHULLER

I've interacted with world leaders and with Americans from all walks of life; I've traveled to over fifty countries. But my most treasured moments are those spent with my family. I've been blessed with the stability and love of Marilyn and our three children. I grew up with loving, supportive parents and caring siblings. It's relatively easy for me to prefer my own home to anywhere else. I delight in the company of my wife and children.

DAN QUAYLE

"God sets the lonely in families."

PSALM 68:6

Call it a clan, call it a network, call it a tribe, call it a family. Whatever you call it, whoever you are, you need one.

JANE HOWARD

When my parents decided, five years ago, to move onto the farm where Wellspring meets, joining the two other families who were there, they built a log cabin as their house. They shipped in logs from two Wisconsin cabins which German settlers had built in the 1800s. The family congregated to do the building, and we invited anyone to join us if they wanted to be part of the project. Each day someone new showed up, sometimes whole families at a time, who wanted to lift logs into position, drill holes for the wooden pegs that held them tight, nail down shingles, put up dry wall, hang curtains, wallpaper. We were the closet thing to an Amish barn-raising that you could get in Kansas . . .

TIM BASCOM

Michael is perhaps the most eloquent member of an eloquent family. He was able to contribute several insights on parenthood beyond the many already presented. "My parents have always been very focused with us, and they always knew what they wanted out of family life," Michael says. "They always ingrained in us what it meant to be a family and what love was, not necessarily telling us but demonstrating it. I think their idea of family was grafted onto us. They wanted to make sure that love was included, and everybody had— I hesitate to say a job, but a role. They've always been supportive and loving, always wanted us to be successful. I think that is partly why we are who we are—because there was always love and respect between the two of them."

DAN QUAYLE

The pleasure of belonging to a family is a treasure indeed. Each person needs a place where he or she belongs . . . You and I gravitate to a place that we can call our own, a place where we can hang our hat, where we can live in privacy. Where I can be me! We naturally are pulled toward a person or group of persons whom we can trust, and where we are accepted as we really are. This, then, is the joy of belonging to a family. We can relax in a private place, whether it is a tent or a tower, a condominium, a cottage, or a castle, with people who love us as we are.

ARVELLA SCHULLER

To be rooted is perhaps the most important and least recognized need of the human soul.

SIMONE WEIL

A happy family is but an earlier heaven.

JOHN BOWRING

Fifty years ago when Chris and I were married, we founded our family on prayer. Through the years we have experienced disasters, deaths, rebellions, and going to war. But the fabric of undergirding prayer we wove has stood the test of time; God Himself has been crisscrossed through the fabric of our home.

EVELYN CHRISTENSON

Although Jesus called His followers to a relationship that was beyond that of family ties, He Himself recognized the family as the ultimate ideal of relational bonding. There was nothing else—no other concept—that had the verbal force to illustrate the loyalty, the love, the close connectedness, as that of the family.

RUTH A. TUCKER

The family that prays together stays together.

The family, grounded on marriage freely contracted, monogamous and indissoluble, is and must be considered the first and essential cell of human society.

POPE JOHN XXIII

On quieter evenings the girls sewed or made up their own games like Smiling Mary, a card game like whist, while Lily or Louisa read aloud the latest novel. And no doubt the family kept to the Victorian pattern of family prayers, hands clasped together, morning or evening or both, with grace before meals. Politeness was paramount. The rule of the house was "Thou shalt not call thy nurse a Beast."

GREVILLE MACDONALD

Repentance, that is to say, is but the homesickness of the soul, and the uninterrupted and watching care of the parent is the fairest earthly type of the unfailing forgiveness of God. The family is, to the mind of Jesus, the nearest of human analogies to the divine order which it was his mission to reveal.

FRANCIS GREENWOOD PEABODY

When we are considering society from any other point of view than the economic, we can all see well enough that, of all its institutions, the family is after all the institution that matters most.

ELEANOR RATHBONE (1924)

While Jesus was suffering the excruciating pain of crucifixion, His thoughts and concerns were for His mother. Who would look after her when He was gone? In that moment of utter anguish, the privilege—and burden—fell on John, His beloved disciple. They were both agonizing with Him at the foot of the cross. To His mother, He said, "Woman, behold thy son." To John, "Behold thy mother." St. Ambrose referred to these words as: Christ's "family testament."

JEAN CANTINAT

Families are ancient institutions. Since humans crossed the savannas in search of food, our families have been unique . . . Unlike monkeys, who can run around within hours of birth and are self-sufficient within a few months, it takes humans in even the simplest environments more than a decade to be independent of parents. Homosapiens needs families to survive.

MARY PIPHER, PH.D.

For six months I was privileged to live with the poor in the Philippines, learning from them . . . I lived in a little plywood shack on stilts. If you followed the ditch that ran under the house, full of bottle caps and human waste, it led to a filthy river called, paradoxically, the San Juan. The squatters lived there only because no one else wanted to be so close to so much toxic waste, particularly since the San Juan flooded almost every year.

The Gasces family gave me a fourth of their one-room home, keeping the rest for themselves and their two little boys, Tom and Jojit. We built two plywood walls and a narrow door so I could have privacy; when I lay down on my cot, I could touch all four walls at once. But even this tight little room was a luxury most squatters did not have—a space of my own.

TIM BASCOM

We offer our thanks to thee
for sending thy only Son to die for us all.
In a world divided by color bars,
how sweet a thing it is to know
that in thee we all belong to one family.

A BANTU PRAYER FROM AFRICA

Family meals were the foundation of communication in the Jordan home. We saw dinnertime not just as the source of necessary nutrition but as a chance to keep in touch with each other's lives, maintain family ties, and nurture relationships by communicating with each other.

DELORIS JORDAN

We have lived and loved together,
Through many changing years;
We have shared each other's gladness,
We have wept each other's tears.

I have never known a sorrow
That was long unsoothed by thee;
For thy smile can make a summer,
Where darkness else would be.

And let us hope the future
As the past has been, will be;
I will share with thee thy sorrow,
And thou thy smiles with me.

ANONYMOUS

The morning snuggles in bed; the springtime walks when baby made three; the diaper changes done family-style, with my husband making funny faces for our son's delight. These were the times when we absorbed the central fact of our lives; that we had been transformed. We were a family.

BETTE-JANE RAPHAEL

A friend told me about her six-year-old grandson who was helping his father puzzle out how to mend a broken lamp while his grandfather looked on.

"Do you know how talented your father is at fixing things?" the proud grandfather asked.

Yes," the boy said with a serious expression on his face, "but do you know what he's really best at?"

"What?" the surprised grandfather asked.

"He's best at loving."

SUE BENDER

# HOME

IS WHERE WE ARE
FIRST LOVED

A man tells an interesting experience from his youth: "When I was around thirteen and my brother was ten, Dad promised to take us to the circus. But at lunch time there was a phone call. Some urgent business required his attention downtown. My brother and I braced ourselves for the disappointment. Then we heard him say, 'No, I won't be down. It will have to wait.'

"When he came back to the table Mom smiled, 'The circus keeps coming back you know.'

"'Yes, I know,' said Dad, 'but childhood doesn't.'"

JOHN M. DRESCHER

As apostles of Christ we could have been a burden to you, but we were gentle among you, like a mother caring for her little children.

**1 THESSALONIANS 2:7**

For Ray and me, *being there* was always an essential and required parenting strategy. It didn't begin with college basketball games or with our fourth child. It was a lifelong commitment we made to each of our five children.

**DELORIS JORDAN**

As I write these words, the three most important women in my life are sleeping upstairs. Before I sleep for the night, I will peek in on my daughters. I will walk over to Kendall's little bed and put the quilt over her, because she doesn't realize how cold it gets in this old house, and she'll wake up freezing if I don't put that extra blanket on her. I'll stop by Erin's bed, and I'll do the same thing I do every night. I'll reach out my hand and put it softly across her hair, feel her breath, and wonder whether I had anything to do with making something so incredibly beautiful, so nearly perfect. Then I'll look to God. "Help me, Lord. I still don't get this fathering daughters thing."

JACK SCHREUR

Time alone for parent and child is difficult in a big family, but Susanna [Wesley] was well-organized, and private time was a high priority with her: "On Monday, I talk with Molly; on Tuesday with Hetty; Wednesday with Nancy; Thursday with Jack; Friday with Patty; Saturday with Charles; and with Emily and Suky together on Sunday."

JOHN W. DRAKEFORD

Little things matter. If your motive is right, even nose-wiping can result in eternal rewards. And that, dear friends, is nothing to sneeze at!

LORRAINE PINTUS

Each night as my parents put me to bed, I was reminded of God's care. Over my bed hung a plaque of a little girl in a tiny rowboat out on the ocean. She was surrounded by a dark night sprinkled with stars. Under the scene were the words, "Dear God, my little boat and I are on Your open sea. Please guide us safely through the waves, my little boat and me." As I gazed at the plaque, it amazed me that the girl was apparently not afraid. "Wow!" I thought. "That little girl really trusts God—but I wonder where her parents are? I'm glad mine are here."

JONI EARECKSON TADA

One day as I went into my office and sat down to start working, I noticed that on one of my scratch pads one of my daughters had written, "I love you, Dad," and signed her name. That warmed my heart!

JIM CONWAY

Animal crackers, and cocoa to drink,
That is the finest of suppers, I think;
When I'm grown up and can have what I please
I think I shall always insist upon these.

CHRISTOPHER MORLEY

One day when I was in my teens, angry at my own father, I asked my grandpa how he could forgive my dad for the things he had done, for the shame and embarrassment he had brought to the family. My grandpa's reply was simple, "He was always my son. I forgave him without thinking about it. I never held anything against him. He was my son, and I loved him."

JACK SCHREUR

The night my first child was born, the nurse tapped on my door at 4:00 A.M. and woke me for his first feeding. After she disappeared into the darkness of the hospital, I gathered him close to my breasts. It was our first meeting alone. I looked into his face, and in the silence, with his little chest pressed against mine, I suddenly felt his heart beating on my skin. It was one of the most vivid moments of my life. It seemed his heart entered mine and beat inside it.

SUE MONK KIDD

God bless Mama and Papa, my brothers and sisters, and all my friends. And now, God, do take care of Yourself, for if anything should happen to You, we'd all be in the soup.

E. STANLEY JONES, QUOTING A CHILD'S PRAYER

Oh, the comfort of Daddy's lap! The strength of those big arms to hug away the cares of the world. The gentleness of a fatherly finger to wipe away tears. In Daddy's lap, life's battle vanished. Nothing existed but the warmth and nearness of the father.

LORRAINE PINTUS

Seeing the world through the eyes of small children also increases my appreciation for the creation. The wonder of a lightning bug, the beauty of a butterfly, the taste of an ice cream cone, the uniqueness of a leaf or a snowflake—all take on new meaning as I see them through the delighted eyes of a child.

PHYLLIS LEPEAU

I knew I was loved by my father more than anything in the world. I can't say I've grown up without faults, but one of the neatest things in my life has been to know that my father loves me more than anything else!

**TIM VANDE GUCHTE**

Whenever I hear my own words and ideas being expressed by my adult children, it thrills my soul as a mother. I have to say, "Thank you, Lord. They really are listening. It didn't just go in one ear and out the other. We truly were *communicating*.

**DELORIS JORDAN**

I looked at my children's picture this morning
I miss them so
the dailiness of living in the same house
the time when we were a happy family
together . . .

I find myself relating to them now
no longer as a family group
but one to one
to each as an individual
exchanging letters with each
discovering the ways in which
each relationship is unique
to be understood, shared, and fostered
in particular ways
not fearing the diversity
but enjoying it
the parental role abides
the personal knowing deepens
I long to be known by my children

I stand alone by the salt block
and think of each child
pray for each one
and for myself
not without tears
and smiles

ROBERT A. RAINES

Our children never outreach God's reach. This doesn't mean they won't go astray. This doesn't mean they won't mess up their lives. But sometimes we forget God is omnipotent, omnipresent, omniscient, and eternal. Our children can run but God knows where they are, and God's watching over them. I remember praying, "Lord, help me discipline this boy." He could get into more mischief when he was little. God never speaks out loud to me, but I know when He's spoken. "Love him more," He told me.

RUTH GRAHAM

I did my stint during the night, feeding them and changing them when they were babies. I got up at 2:00 A.M. and looked forward to it as much as I looked forward to the nights that I would sleep. We would take turns— one night mine, one night was my wife's. Then it kind of evolved from there and we'd just do stuff as a family. We did everything together. Our kids' friends would call up on a weekend and say, 'Do you want to do this?' or, 'Do you want to go here?' And the answer usually was, 'Well, my mom and dad and I are going to go here and there this weekend.'"

DOUG LAPINSKI

More and more children these days are moving back home a decade or two after they have stopped being children because the schools have been making the mistake of teaching Robert Frost, who said, "Home is the place where, when you go there, they have to take you in." Why don't they teach *You Can't Go Home Again* instead?

BILL COSBY

If we're not careful, we can delude ourselves into thinking that growing up is hopping from hill to hill, never taking time to notice the valleys in between. But life is more about the valleys than the hills. In my advanced years, I've sort of lost memory of the hills, but I remember the ordinary days, a smile, a casual word, a pat on the back; the day Dad did just a little extra for me and forgot as soon as he had done it; the day Mom took a moment to doctor a hurt that wasn't all that hurt, but needed emotional attention instead. These are the good old days that keep creeping back into my conscious being and dictating attitudes and emotions that I know are proper half a century later.

CLIFF SCHIMMELS

# HOME

Is the foundation
for the person we
become

My father and mother always had a good sense of humor. Sometimes he could make her laugh so hard she cried. Yet you could also see the other end of the spectrum. I've always said this: "In marriage you love one another but sometimes you just don't like each other." My family values were taught growing up. My parents set the example; I am a part of my parents, figuratively and literally. *They've made me into someone my wife could love.*

### TONY DE LA ROSA

In this family life . . . Mary more than anyone else has helped me find God in the commonplace and see him patiently working in my life. She has often put her finger on a sore spot of my life that needs healing. And while I've sometimes responded with a vehement defense of my behavior, I have on more than one occasion realized she was God's answer to my desire to know him better.

RONALD E. WILSON

Not long ago, at my five-year-old daughter's request, we went through photographs of her since birth and arranged them in an album to "tell her story." . . . Each time we look at these photos, I realize how deeply my daughter trusts me to be a reservoir of memory for her, to recall the things too shadowy for her to recall and to interpret the cycles of her young life.

ANNE PELLOWSKI

These commandments that I give you today are to be upon your hearts. Impress them on your children. Talk about them when you sit at home and when you walk along the road, when you lie down and when you get up.

DEUTERONOMY 6:6-7

The Christian home is the Master's workshop where the processes of character-molding are silently, lovingly, faithfully and successfully carried on.

RICHARD MONCKTON MILNES

The rearing of children was one of the most important of these [traditional family] functions. Since slave parents were primarily responsible for training their children, they could cushion the shock of bondage for them, help them to understand their situation, teach them values different from those their masters tried to instill in them, and give them a referent for self-esteem other than their master.

JOHN W. BLASSINGAME

For me and my siblings, the family we grew up with gave us our perspective.

. . . It's a wonderfully messy arrangement, in which relationships overlap, underlie, support, and oppose one another. It didn't always come together easily nor does it always stay together easily. It's known very good times and very bad ones. It has held together, often out of shared memories and hopes, sometimes out of the lure of my sisters' cooking, and sometimes out of sheer stubbornness. And like the world itself, our family is renewed by each baby.

MARGE KENNEDY

On Christmas Eve our whole extended family gets together, and after dinner we read in unison the Christmas story from Luke 2. Then we discuss what Jesus would like for a birthday present. The children decide (sometimes with help) that He wants our hearts. But our hearts are dirty, and we can't give someone a dirty birthday present. So, under each plate is a red heart with a black sticker on it. We have a quiet time when people ask God for forgiveness for the "black spot." Then they peel it off, throw it into the blazing fireplace, and then put their clean heart in a box wrapped like a birthday present. When everyone is finished, the children put the box under the Christmas tree and sing, "Happy Birthday, Dear Jesus." It's a sweet, introspective time that I treasure and the girls love to set up.

JAN JOHNSON

That faithful servant of Yours, my mother, came to You in my behalf with more tears than most mothers shed at a child's funeral. Her faith in You had made plain to her that I was spiritually dead. And You heard her, Lord, You heard her. You didn't ignore the tears that fell from her eyes and watered the earth everywhere she prayed.

ST. AUGUSTINE

The person who influenced my life most as far as my education and character are concerned was my mother. Even though she only finished the fifth grade, she was the wisest person and the greatest teacher I've ever known. By word and deed she taught with hundreds of little "sermonettes" that creep into my conversations, speeches, and writings to this day.

ZIG ZIGLAR

Family gatherings are often designed around a special event—a birth or a death, a birthday or an anniversary. And sometimes there's an urge to incorporate into these occasions many of the same rituals our parents and even grandparents enacted. The carving of the roast, the ritual of grace or hands around the table with each person squeezing the hand of the next person, the ritual of decorations; who gets the first piece of cake, who makes a wish, a toast, who sings a song. These gatherings can't happen every day, yet we treasure such moments as truly special events . . . While you can't save living just for these moments alone, when they do happen the rest of your life is touched.

ALEXANDRA STODDARD

The one lesson my dad taught me: If you're going to do anything in life, do it right.

MONTY CRALLEY

The ordinary arts we practice every day at home are of more importance to the soul than their simplicity might suggest.

THOMAS MOORE

Listen you children who are going to table. Wash your hands and cut your nails. Do not sit at the head of the table; This is reserved for the father of the house. Do not commence eating until a blessing is said. Dine in God's name And permit the eldest to begin first. Proceed in a disciplined manner. Do not snort or smack like a pig. Do not reach violently for bread, Lest you may knock over a glass. Do not cut bread on your chest . . . Do not elbow the person sitting next to you. Sit up straight; be a model of gracefulness . . . Silently praise and thank God for the food He has graciously provided And you have received from His fatherly hand . . .

HANS SACHS, SHOEMAKER

At Jan's house they begin every November 1 to focus on being thankful by getting out their "Thanksgiving Tree." It is a branch set in plaster of Paris on which each of them daily hangs a leaf, praying thanks to God for the thing or person whose name they have written on the leaves. "But," says Jan, "the thing that makes us really thankful is keeping the leaves in a baggie, and getting them out the next year and seeing what God has done in answer to those prayers."

EVELYN CHRISTENSON

Mom never took a course in parenting. She never heard those neo-Freudian theories about child rearing. I am sure that the "experts" in the field of child psychology could find many flaws in her practices. All I know is that she was always there. And she believed in me. And she modeled for me that missionary work is the best thing anyone can do. That's not a bad legacy for the daughter of Italian immigrants who had to drop out of school when she was nine years old. I hope that somehow she knows her dream lives on.

TONY CAMPOLO

But have you ever noticed that many of the memories you have about the good times and the good lessons you had with your parents were in those unintentional moments when neither party stopped to realize, "Wow, this is an eternal learning experience we're having here!" Our parents didn't mean to be good teachers. They just were, and to think that they did it all by accident!

CLIFF SCHIMMELS

In a man whose childhood has known caresses and kindness, there is always a fiber of memory that can be touched to gentle issues.

GEORGE ELIOT

Husband and wife characteristically accept each other as they are. Their faith in each other's regard for them is not based on their own worth or right, but on the other's acceptance of them just as they are. It is hard to think of any other relationship (except perhaps within a religious community) where acceptance could be so unreserved, so productive of mutual health and growth.

CATHERINE DE HUECK DOHERTY

I can still see that room in the twilight and that large bearded figure with the great shoulders bowed above me, and hear the broken voice and the tenderness in it. I like best to think of him that way. Before then and after I saw him holding the attention of thou- sands of people, but asking for forgiveness of his unconsciously disobedient little boy for having spoken harshly seemed to me then and seems now a finer and a greater thing, and to it I owe more than I owe to any of his sermons. For to this I am indebted for an understanding of the meaning of the Fatherhood of God, and a belief in the love of God had its beginning that night in my childish mind.

PAUL MOODY

When I was growing up in the 1940s and 1950s, life was much harder in many ways than it is today. We dreamed about the appliances and home furnishings and gadgets pictured in the Sears and Roebuck catalog, but they were beyond the reach of a poor farm family. Our "bathroom" was an outhouse, and we took our Saturday night baths in the kitchen in a big washtub right near the old wood stove. We washed our clothes with a ringer washer, and milked the cows by hand. It was a simple life back then, and I can sometimes still smell the fresh-mowed hay, hear the bumblebees buzzing in the clover, and see the Holstein cows grazing in the south pasture.

RUTH A. TUCKER

# HOME

---

## CONNECTS THE PAST
## WITH THE PRESENT

There were six of us children, spread over a period of sixteen years, but the oldest three of us remember the Depression. My father earned something in the neighborhood of twenty-five hundred dollars a year. We lived in a "double" house in what is now a slum area of Germantown with a pocket-handkerchief-size yard that seemed to produce hairpins and pearl buttons more readily than grass. We did not know that we were "poor," for in those days the door bell was often rung by peddlers selling shoelaces, needles and thread, or clothes line props. My mother told us not to buy anything but just to give them a dime from the tithe box. My parents were strict tithers, and the box of dimes in the living room table drawer was a portion of the money given to God. Because we were always in the position of givers, we thought we were well off.

ELISABETH ELLIOT

I have been reminded of your sincere faith, which first lived in your grandmother Lois and in your mother Eunice and, I am persuaded, now lives in you also.

2 TIMOTHY 1:5

I know it is the happy experiences that we remember that still bind us together. I know that when I laughed with my children our love was enlarged and a door swung open for our doing many more things together.

JOHN M. DRESCHER

My dad understood our need for recess and still does his best to bring a sense of play and laughter to his fathering. We laughed loud and long in our family, and I am convinced that our sense of play has held us together during difficult times. I know that my father's intuitive understanding of the need for recess is one of the reasons why I loved him so much when I was a boy. My dad celebrates life and takes everybody near him along for the ride if they will hang on. That has been a tremendous source of strength in our relationship and has been a key building block for many other fathers and sons.

JACK SCHREUR

Back in the good old days, one of the prerequisites for motherhood was to be board-certified in family medical practice and have credentials in veterinary medicine as well, if the family had pets. Although mom's clinic and apothecary were not as well stocked and didn't smell the same as the official ones, we nevertheless recovered from most of our maladies with only minor lasting effects.

To achieve family health, Mom used three kinds of treatment: packs, potions, and soaks. Sometimes she would prescribe a single dosage, but most of the time she used all three together ... Packs could be concocted from about anything, as long as they met the one criterion of smelling bad. Of course, that was Mom's way of heading off epidemics of contagious diseases. When she got that pack on you, it didn't matter whether you went out in public. As bad as you smelled, no one was coming close enough to catch anything anyway.

CLIFF SCHIMMELS

Our own house on Bush's place had three rooms and a kitchen. With a couple of aunts, uncles and some cousins living there, too, our family varied between 12 and 15 people all the time. There were only five beds. So we younger children had to sleep head to foot in a bed— several at the head and some more at the foot—eight of us together on a shuck bed.

Breakfast at grandma's place was plain— flour gravy and cornbread. Grandma would heat up flour in a skillet with a dab of lard and brown it a bit for flavor. Then she added water to make the gravy. Sometimes she had a piece of pork or salt back to add to it.

Lunch would be simple, especially when we'd be in school and have to take something with us— usually a bit of corn bread or some biscuits with homemade jelly.

JOHN PERKINS

My father would tell stories till the tears of laughter rolled down my mother's face. We children enjoyed them and enjoyed one another. It was a happy home. We knew we were loved, we knew the Lord was the head of the house, we knew where the lines were drawn, we were safe.

**ELISABETH ELLIOT**

Now that I've gotten to the place in life where the pace has slowed a bit and the battle doesn't rage so urgently, I've had time to assess my life, and I've concluded that my parents knew quite a lot about the science of parenting.

**CLIFF SCHIMMELS**

When I was in junior high I played football for my school. I was one of the smallest kids on the team and was not a particularly good player. Every Saturday evening I would look into the stands and see my dad sitting there, and Saturday after Saturday I didn't play. Yet he was still there. Finally, in the next-to-last game of the season we were undefeated and were pummeling a visiting team. I was put into the game for the final two minutes as a defensive back. The runner came my way, and I managed to grab him by the shoe. Two other players joined in, and we managed to bring him down. I had shared in a tackle! I looked quickly to the stands and saw my father smiling, with his thumb pointed up in the air, sharing in my brief and modest moment of glory because he was committed to me.

JACK SCHREUR

When I was a boy, I told people that my father was stronger than anyone else in the world. He was a handsome man in those days. He had a curl of hair at the middle of his forehead, and brown eyes, and a pulsing muscle in his jaw. And he loved me.

So I would go out on the front porch and roar to the neighborhood: "My daddy's arm is as strong as trucks! The strongest man in the world."

WALTER WANGERIN, JR.

In some wealthy European or Asian families of the eighteenth and nineteenth centuries, there was a special servant or family member whose designated job was to tell stories at night, before the household went to sleep. If the head of household (or someone else of authority in the house) had insomnia, the teller was expected to get up and begin telling soothing, sleep-induced tales. In my family, it was my oldest sister, Angie, who told me and my sisters bedtime stories.

ANNE PELLOWSKI

The oldest boy sat in the back seat behind Dad, the oldest daughter sat directly behind Mom, and any younger children in the family scheme sat on the hump in the middle. That was their punishment for not being the firstborn of the gender, and it was considerable punishment, because the humps were high and the roads were bumpy. As a natural born hump-rider myself, I remember praying that God would let me grow up and never sit in the middle again.

CLIFF SCHIMMELS

I grew up watching how the extended family took care of each other. One of the delightful stories told was how the Rodier kids (my mother's family of seven children) would fight among themselves, but heaven help the kids who would attack a Rodier. The Rodiers stuck together to protect their own.

WILLIAM F. NERIN

Every detail of school and play came up on the bedtime screen. Nothing was hidden from Mama. As she tucked me in, she always said, "Look at me, Margaret. Is there anything you need to tell me before we talk to God?" Knowing her secret line to God, the confession poured out, and forgiveness followed. Sleep was sweet.

MARGARET JENSEN

The first time I came across my grandmother's graduation ring, I was about seven. I begged my mother to let me wear it. This went on for years until the ring finally moved from my mother's dresser drawer to my right hand when I was 16. She swore I'd lose it. I swore I wouldn't.

During my years of wearing it, I have felt an incredible connectedness to my grandmother that surprises me.

Someday I hope to give it to my daughter. At age five, she's already expressed interest in it. I told her she'd just lose it. She swears she wouldn't. We've agreed she can have it when she's 16.

I had it appraised once. It's worth about 20 dollars. And much, much more.

MARGE KENNEDY

My parents surrounded me with the Gospel and nestled me in their love for it. I often happened in on my father as he sat alone with the Bible, tears streaming down his cheeks at the beauty of some revelation. In our home, prayer was a natural response to problems and crises as well as good news and celebrations. My parents were verbal about their relationship with God, with each other, with us children, and with others. "I love you" was heard daily, not only when we were having family hugs, but also when we were having family worship.

My parents also gave me a sense of humor, and believe me, survival in a parsonage often depended on our ability to laugh. Daddy, for example, doubled over with laughter when we told him he had declared that "Judas is a carrot," and we all got a hearty chuckle from the prayer meeting in which a dear old saint testified that "my head hurt and I asked the Lord to take it away—and he did!"

GLORIA GAITHER

When my son was ten and my daughter four, we camped at Blue Stem Lake. In the afternoon Zeke landed a twelve-inch bass and Sara rescued a frog. While my husband played his guitar under a cottonwood, I lay reading on the shore. For dinner we ate hamburgers and beans. In the dark, we roasted marshmallows around a fire. We listened to cicadas and the motor of a small boat. A moon the shape and color of a pumpkin rose over the lake. Sara snuggled into her father and said a line so beautiful that I can quote it fifteen years later: "I'm melting into richness."

MARY PIPHER, PH.D.

No family is immune from tension and problems. We had our allotment of sickness death, and disappointment. Our family experienced two very sad deaths at Christmas—each a touching story of its own. But life was also compassionate in allowing happiness to be interspersed—the part of home we remember.

RUTH HACKMAN

Even though we were poor growing up, we weren't poor in spirit.

JIM BURNS

One of the most meaningful birthday prayers of our family was prayed in July 1986 by my mother, Grandma Moss. All of her great grandchildren had gathered at a cottage on Lake Michigan for a rare combined big birthday party. Those great grandchildren were very precious to Grandma Moss, and she had lived sacrificially for them and her grandchildren and her children all of her life. So we were thrilled to have her there at age ninety-one to pray for that collection of her great grandchildren, captured for us all on video tape.

Holding baby Crista on one hip, she surveyed her rich family possessions, and raised her voice to the God she knew so well. "As we look to Thee at this time, God, we have so many things to thank You for." Then, flowing from the depths of her being came, "We begin, Lord, by thanking Thee that Thou hast privileged us to be together today. So many of our family are here . . ."

Next came her deep lifelong goal for herself and goal for all her family line. "And we want to make Thee first in our lives, and we want to please Thee in everything we do and everything we say."

And, before thanking God for the wonderful food and all the hands that had prepared it, Grandma Moss prayed the last thing she ever prayed in public for anyone. *Her blessing for her offspring.*

"And, God, we just ask Thee to bless each one and bless these, especially these that are having their birthdays. God, we ask Thee to come and bless their lives, and help them to grow up to be wonderful Christian men and women. And we'll give Thee the praise and the glory. Amen." At the end of that week Grandma Moss dropped dead of a massive stroke. That birthday prayer was her final blessing!

EVELYN CHRISTENSON

As Grandma Mac unwrapped her gifts, someone asked her this pensive question: "Would you tell us what is the happiest memory of your ninety years?" It did seem a natural question right then. So we stilled ourselves and waited.

What would she say? (You should know that she'd been a widow for seventeen years. Because her husband was a career officer in the military, they had traveled the world together. "Several times clear around," she'd told us often. He'd also invested wisely, and that being true, she lived with another blessing: She'd been able to buy almost anything one little lady could want when she wanted it. Idyllic background really, for the recollection of memories.)

But tonight there was no need for recollection. Without one moment's hesitation she said, "Oh, that's easy. It's all those times Louis and I would sit on the back porch and visit."

CHARLIE W. SHEDD

We didn't have any money growing up, but that isn't the essential. We had happiness.

HELEN CASEY

By profession I am a soldier and take pride in that fact. But I am prouder to be a father. My hope is that my son, when I am gone, will remember me not from battle, but in the home, repeating with him one simple prayer, "Our Father which art in heaven."

GENERAL DOUGLAS MACARTHUR

Adolescence is not always an easy time, and my teen years were probably less easy than most people's. But my father never gave up on me. When I was rude to him or treated him badly, he never quit loving me; and somehow through that difficult time in my life I loved my father more deeply than I ever had as a child. I no longer thought of him as perfect. Instead, I became aware of a man who lived what he said he believed and did what he said he would do. As a teenager I fought with my father. We argued about music, about what kind of person I was, about girls, and about church. But he never lied to me and never went back on his word. He never made me feel stupid. He listened to my ideas and then discussed them with me. He treated me like a human being.

JACK SCHREUR

Peace, unto this house, I pray,
Keep terror and despair away;
Shield it from evil and let sin
Never find lodging room within.
May never in these walls be heard
The hateful or accusing word . . .

Lord, this humble house we'd keep
Sweet with play and calm with sleep.
Help us so that we may give
Beauty to the lives we live.
Let Thy love and let Thy grace
Shine upon our dwelling place.


EDGAR A. GUEST

# ACKNOWLEDGEMENTS

Reasonable care has been taken to trace ownership of the materials quoted from in this book, and to obtain permission to use copyrighted materials, when necessary.

*A Farthing Oak – Meditations From the Mountain,* Robert Raines, 1982, Crossroad Publishing Co., New York, New York. All rights reserved.

*The American Family,* Dan Quayle and Diane Medved, 1996, Harper Collins Publishing, New York, New York. All rights reserved.

*The Comfort Trap,* Tim Bascom, 1993, InterVarsity Press, Westmont, Illinois. All rights reserved.

*If I Were Starting My Family Again* by John M. Drescher. © Good Books.

*Pictures of Home* by Colin Thompson. Reprinted with the permission of Simon & Schuster Books for Young Readers, an imprint of Simon & Schuster Children's Publishing Division. Copyright © 1992 Colin Thompson.

*Plain and Simple,* Sue Bender, 1989, Harper San Francisco, San Francisco, California. All rights reserved.

*The Positive Family* by Arvella Schuller. Copyright © 1982 by Arvella Schuller. Used by permission of Doubleday, a division of Bantam Doubleday Dell Publishing Group, Inc.

*Simple Abundance: A Daybook of Comfort and Joy* by Sarah Ban Breathnach, 1995, Warner Books, New York, New York.